Tallinn
a town of living history

PHOTO
TOUR

Text: Kristina Porgasaar
Translation: Aliis Hazlehurst Palo
Photos: Ainur Kruuse, Ain Avik,
Malev Toom, Toomas Tuul, Toomas Volmer
Design: Stella F.
Editor in chief: Ainur Kruuse
Publishing house: Grenader Grupp OÜ
Printed in the Greif printing house
ISBN 9949-11-61-0

The limestone plateau known as Toompea, meaning dome hill, is a perfect defensive site for a fortress – a stretch of land high up on a limestone plateau bordered by steep slopes on each side. There has been a settlement on the site of Tallinn for more than a thousand years, with a port near the sea, a market close by and a castle higher up the hill. It is thought that this was the rocky site that the Arab geographer al-Idrisi marked on his world map under the name of Qlwry in 1154. According to legend, the hill was heaped up by Linda, the widow of the Estonian epic hero Kalev, as an eternal memorial to her beloved husband.

In 1219 the Danes led by King Valdemar II laid siege to Tallinn. Legend has it that in the midst of the battle against the Estonians, the Archbishop of Lund stood in the middle of the battlefield with his arms to the heavens, praying for a Danish victory over the pagans. As long as the man of God was able to hold up his arms, the fighting favoured the Danes, but when fatigue made him drop them, the Estonians got the upper hand. At a crucial moment, a flag displaying a white cross against a red background fell from the sky and a heavenly voice said: "Hold it high and you will be victorious!" The Danes won with the help of the flag, which is still the national flag of Denmark. The Estonians also saw the falling flag and the same image was used on the coat of arms of Tallinn. Both can be seen today in the Danish King's Garden.

Coat of arms of Tallinn and the flag of Denmark in the Danish King's Garden.

Toompea Castle: Pilsticker Tower on the left, Tall Hermann on the right.

Interior view of the Dome Church. ▲

In order to strengthen their position the victors began to build a new fortress on the site of the former one. The Estonians called it the Danish Fortress (*Taani linnus*). This was later shortened to Tallinn and gave the city its name. The construction of a church probably began around the same time, and in 1240 the Dome Church was consecrated as St. Mary's Cathedral of the Estonian diocese. The coats of arms of the Baltic-German nobility, members of the Estonian Knighthood, decorate the church, the oldest of which dates back to 1686. Many sarcophagi and tombstones have also been preserved, the most beautiful being the tombstone of the Swedish army leader Pontus de la Gardie and his wife of royal blood Sophia Gyllenhielm.

In the course of the crusade proclaimed by Pope Celestine III, the Germans arrived in Tallinn in 1227. They seized the fortress, drove out the Danes and built a new one, which today is known as the Toompea Castle. Most of it dates back to the 13-14th century, to the rule of the Teutonic Order, but all subsequent rulers have added to it. After the Great Northern War (1700-1721) the Empress of Russia, Catherine II, ordered the construction of a provincial government building here. In the course of the reconstruction that began in 1767, the castle, standing empty at the time, received a late Baroque palace-like façade. The Expressionist style building of the Estonian parliament was built in the castle yard between 1920 and 1922.

TOOMPEA

During the Soviet era the Supreme Soviet of the Estonian Republic was located here, and today it is again the site of the Parliament of Estonia. Despite changes a large part of the castle has retained its initial look, including several towers. The highest of these is Pikk (Tall) Hermann, on which the Estonian flag flies.

The newest church in the Old Town, the Alexander Nevsky Cathedral, is also located on Toompea. Modelled on Russian churches of the 17th century, it was completed in 1900. The interior is decorated with a gilded iconostasis and numerous icons. The eye-catching mosaics above the entrances are rare in Estonia. There are eleven bells in the church towers, the most powerful of which weighs 15 tonnes and is the biggest in the Nordic countries. This Orthodox Church falls within the Moscow Patriarchate, and the current Patriarch Alexy II (whose secular name is Aleksei Ridiger) comes from Tallinn.

Alexander Nevsky Cathedral.

Toompea Castle, the former building of the provincial government.

Dome Church (St. Mary's Cathedral).

Buildings at the beginning of Kohtu street.

In addition to the castle and the church, numerous residences of the former aristocracy are located here. These were built on the steep slope side and form a semi-circle around the church. The buildings in the Classicist style were built after the fire of 1684. The most representative one is the Knighthood House, used for meetings and court hearings, which gave the name Kohtu, meaning Court, to the nearby street. The Baltic-German gentry spent most of their time in their countryside estates but in the social season – from Christmas to Easter – they lived in town. Today the town palaces have new owners: the house decorated with pillars at Kohtu 2, which was once owned by the polar explorer Eduard von Toll, contains luxury flats; Bernhard Otto Jacob von Uexküll's home next door is now the property of the Embassy of Finland; the house at Kohtu 6, built for Ewald Alexander von Ungern-Sternberg in the French-style houses the Academy of Sciences, while the neighbouring house, modelled on the main building of the University of Tartu, and once owned by the Kaulbars family, now belongs to the state.

For more than eight centuries the Town Hall Square has been the meeting point of the town. Nowadays concerts, plays, fairs and festivals, and the annual Tallinn Old Town Days take place here. High-ranking guests are also received here, people socialise in the street cafes, and since 1441 a Christmas tree decorates the square every winter.

In medieval times there were traders in the square: shoemakers' workshops were located near Kinga (Shoe) Street; bakeries were located in Saiakang (White Bread Passage) and the general merchants, later lead casters, were located near Kullassepa (Goldsmith) Street. The wealthier merchants built little shops next to the buildings around the square or in the arcade of the Town Hall; only two little kiosks adjacent to the Town Hall are preserved today.

Christmas market on the Town Hall Square, Town Hall in the background.

The most important building is, of course, the Town Hall, which just recently celebrated its six hundredth birthday. The building received its current look after reconstruction work in 1404. The fact that it is the only remaining Town Hall in Gothic style in the Nordic Countries adds to its significance. The representative halls – the Council Hall and the Citizens' Hall – were located on the second floor, the treasury and wine cellar were in the basement, and the attic was used for storage. A weather vane in the shape of a soldier called Old Thomas – one of the best-loved symbols of the capital today – was put on the top of the tower in 1530.

White Bread Passage.

Concert in the Citizens' Hall in the Town Hall.

The town council assembled in the Town Hall. The only guild whose members could be elected to the council was the Great Guild; the fact that both organisations used the same image on their coat of arms – a white cross against a red background – testifies to their close relations. The members of the town council were elected for their lifetime but from time to time they could take a leave of absence from their council responsibilities in order to promote their business.

Several historical traces can be found on the Town Hall Square: the locations of the pillory and Weigh House are marked; a big flat stone marks the spot of the former well and the letter L marks the place where a priest was beheaded, because in a fit of anger he had murdered a tavern's servant girl with an axe. This was the only execution ever carried out within the town walls.

Old Thomas.

L-shaped mark in the pavement.

The town council owned several buildings around the Town Hall Square. The dwelling quarters of the town herald and the Town Council Prison were located behind the Town Hall, the chancellery and the housekeeper's building were on the square. The pharmacy, butcher's shops and others were rented out. Of these, only the Town Council Pharmacy still operates. It is one of the oldest pharmacies in the world, first mentioned as early as 1422. The most successful pharmacist's were the Burcharts from Hungary, who ran the pharmacy for ten generations. During its first years the pharmacy resembled a café, where customers could have a drink and buy sweet cakes. Of course, it also offered medications, which at the time were made of gems, amber oil, powdered unicorn horn etc. By tradition the most popular products – marzipan and claret – are still presented to the town council on St. Thomas' Day as a supplement to the rent.

Symbol of the pharmacy on an old shop sign.

Interior of the Town Council's Pharmacy.

Main commercial street; Viru Gates in the foreground, Viru Hotel in the background.

St. Nicholas' Church.

Tallinn has always been the capital of Estonia, an economic, trade and cultural centre. Although the town has expanded over the centuries, partly by incorporating some of the surrounding areas, the Lower Town is still the heart of the town's life. The actual development of the city into two separate towns – Toompea, the town ruled by the Knighthood, and the Lower Town, which functioned as an independent city-state – began in 1230 when German merchants from Gotland arrived here on the invitation of the Order of the Brothers of the Sword. The town flourished, and the Charter of Lübeck was conferred during the reign of the Danish King Erik IV in 1248. By the end of the same century Tallinn, known at the time as Reval, had become a member of the Hanseatic League. The town saw great economic prosperity in the 14-15th centuries and most of the buildings in the Lower Town date back to that period.

The construction of the churches began in the 13th century. One of the most interesting is the church dedicated by the Germans to St. Nicholas, the patron saint of merchants. Today it houses a museum, one of whose exhibits is the rare 15th century painting "Dance Macabre" by the Lübeck master Bernt Notke. The church dedicated to the Norwegian Saint Olaf was built in the former Scandinavian trade yard. With its 159 metres it was the highest building in the world in the 16th century. Now, after reconstruction, its height is 123,7 metres.

The Holy Spirit Church played an important role in Estonian cultural history. After the Reformation it was passed to an Estonian congregation, and since then, services have been held in Estonian. Several famous pastors have preached here, for example, Johann Koell, whose translation of the catechism published in 1535 is considered to be the first publication in Estonian, and Balthasar Russow, author of the "Livonian Chronicle" (1578). The church houses a number of valuable art relics, including the folding altar (1483) designed by Bernt Notke, the oldest pulpit in town (app. 1597), a balcony with painted scenes from the Bible (17th century), and a clock in the Baroque style (1684), decorating the façade of the church.

St. Olaf's Church.

Interior view of Holy Spirit Church.

The defensive structures of the Old Town are also noteworthy. The Danish Queen Mother Margrethe Sambiria ordered the building of the town wall in 1265, but additional construction work lasted for several centuries. Eventually there were about sixty towers and almost four kilometres of town wall, which was about two meters thick and up to fifteen meters high. Of the defence system only the Toompea Castle and 1,85 km of town wall with towers around the Lower Town have survived. No two towers were alike and even the wall differed in places. Each tower had its own building master, who was responsible for its completion, and for example the Plate and Epping towers were named after them.

The reinforcement of Tallinn intensified at the end of the 17th century during the reign of the Swedish kings, when the defensive structures around the town were expanded. The Ingerian bastion was built in front of the cannon tower Kiek in de Kök and the Skone bastion was built in the port near the Stout Margaret Tower; both received their name from areas that were part of the Swedish kingdom at the time. In the 19th century, bastions lost their military importance and town parks were founded on them.

Part of the town wall with towers called Rope Hill, Plate, Epping and Behind-Grusbeke.

Staircase in front of the Swedish bastion, Tall Hermann in the background.

Stout Margaret Tower.

In medieval times, Pikk (Long) Street was the main street of the town, connecting the port and the market place. The Pikk Jalg (Long Leg), its extension leading to Toompea, is one of the oldest roads in town. The guilds and dwellings of wealthier merchants were located on Pikk Street. Near the former port, at the beginning of the street there are three neighbouring houses with beautiful medieval façades - the Three Sisters, which according to one legend did originally belong to three sisters.

Medieval dwellings were built of stone because of the risk of fire, and their architecture was simple, a high staircase in front, a Gothic arched doorway, and huge quadrangular windows on either side of the door. The low side-buildings were constructed behind the main building and the yard was accessible through an arched passageway. A high gabled façade faced the street. Furnaces were in the cellar, while the ground floor held the living quarters. As Tallinn, a Hanseatic town, had storage rights and could independently regulate trade between east and west, storerooms were built on the upper floors. From the 17th century, some of the storerooms were reconstructed as living rooms and many houses received a new look.

‣ *The Three Sisters on Pikk Street.*

‣ *Short Leg Gateway.*

Long Leg. ‣

House of the Brotherhood of the Black Heads. ▲

The Great Guild was the most important organisation of a medieval Hanseatic town. It was a union of wealthy merchants of German origin, which, in this region, had close connections with the Brotherhood of the Black Heads, an organisation of young single merchants. The brotherhood got its name from its Moorish patron saint, Mauritius. The brothers organised social gatherings and entertainment for the whole town and also formed the cavalry detachment of the town. In order to test their readiness, a bird shooting festival was organised every spring, where the participants had to hit a small parrot figure on a high pole. The winner was proclaimed king and a feast followed. The wealth of the Black Heads was shown by the façade of the Brotherhood's building, completed at the end of the 16th century in the Mannerist style, and by its large collection of paintings and silver, which today can be admired in museums.

Romantic St. Catherine's Passage. ▼

▾ *Moment from the Old Town Days.*

A ccording to legend, every year a little old man comes from Lake Ülemiste to the town and wants to know whether the construction works in Tallinn have been completed. The reply must be that not yet, and that it will take a good few years more. If he is told that the town has been completed, he will at once let the waters of Lake Ülemiste flow from Lasnamäe hill down to the valley and flood the town. On a few occasions the water level of the lake has risen dangerously high but so far the Ülemiste old man has been calmed down and fortunately there is still some free space in the town centre where new buildings can be constructed.

A century ago the edge of the Old Town from Viru Gate to Harju Street was rebuilt; the town wall was partially demolished or covered with higher buildings and the Vabaduse (Liberty) Square was developed. The buildings here are predominantly in a

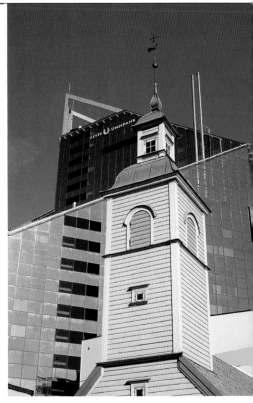

Modern bank building, St. John's Almshouse Church from the 18th century in the foreground.

Opera and ballet theatre "Estonia".

Independence Day parade on Vabaduse Square, ↗
St. John's Church in the background.

The modern city centre. ↖

Performance in "Estonia". ↘

Historicist or Functionalist style, and the most interesting among them are the Neogothic Lutheran John's Church (1867) and an office building with an interesting façade (1932) presently the city government. One of the most important groups of buildings in Estonian history is the headquarters of the National Bank of Estonia, in one of the oldest parts of which the first government of Estonia was formed on February 24, 1918. Nearby is the cultural seat of this country – the opera theatre "Estonia" – completed in 1913, the design of which was entrusted to the Finnish architects A. Lindgren and W. Lönn. Several schools, a clubhouse, a cinema, a hotel and several blocks of flats were also built in the area.

The 23-floor hotel Viru, built in 1972, was the first skyscraper in the centre. Less than ten years later another, hotel Olümpia, was built here for the Olympic games. At the turn of the millennium a boom in high-rise construction began in the town centre: within a couple of years a bank building, hotel Radisson SAS, offices and flats were built. In the near future several other buildings will be constructed here. Tallinn was famous for the highest building in the world – St. Olaf's Church – in the 16th century, and we can see that the desire of the town's architects to scrape the sky has lasted for centuries.

Kadriorg is popular both as a place of leisure and as a residential area, offering a respite from the urban noise and bustle only a short distance from the town centre. The office of the president of Estonia, embassies, museums and cafes are located here and the seaside is just a short walk away. The region was named Kadriorg, meaning Catherine's valley, in honour of Catherine, the wife of Russian Tsar Peter the Great.

The development of Kadriorg began on July 22, 1718 when Peter the Great set the location of the palace and park. Niccolò Michetti, an architect from Rome, designed the palace in the style of an Italian villa. The Baroque main hall stretching through two floors is a real masterpiece, and it has almost entirely retained its original look. Today the foreign art collection of the Art Museum of Estonia is exhibited here, and, among others, works of Dutch, German, Italian, Russian, Austrian and Swiss origin can be seen.

‣ *Office of the President of the Republic of Estonia.*

˅ *View of the Kadriorg Palace from the Upper Garden.*

Main hall of Kadriorg Palace. ➤

Peter the Great's Cottage ➤
in the greenery of the chestnuts.

In addition to the palace, many side-buildings have survived. The former kitchen building near the palace houses the art collection of Johannes Mikkel, which is one of the few private ones in Estonia, collected during the Soviet era. The park pavilion and guesthouse have been turned into restoration workshops. The famous Estonian writer Eduard Vilde (1865-1933) lived for several years in the former estate manager's house. His flat was later turned into his house museum.

The oldest building in Kadriorg is a little white house at the far end of the park, known as Peter the Great's Cottage. Peter the Great bought it with a nearby coppice in 1713 from the town councillor von Drenteln. The summer manor house dates back to the 17th century and has now been turned into a museum, with objects from the era on display.

Kadriorg is being turned into a unique exhibition area, where several new museums are planned. The biggest art museum in Estonia, 'KUMU', designed by the Finnish architect Pekka Vapaavuori is currently being built into the limestone bank. In the near future, exhibition halls of Estonian classical and modern art will be opened here.

The park of Kadriorg covers approximately sixty hectares and features different park styles; around the Swan Pond and next to the palace an 18th century regular park is laid out, while in other parts visitors can wander around in a 19th century natural park and a 20th century public park. The park has always been open to the public and it has become a favourite place for walks both in summer and winter months. The area surrounding the Swan Pond is the most popular, as children more than anyone like to come here to feed the swans and other birds.

The Sea Avenue in Kadriorg Park, Russalka in the background.

Swan Pond.

One of Kadriorg's unusual features is its street names, most of which are named after well-known people from Estonian cultural history. The oldest wooden buildings in Tallinn are located on the street named after the Estonian statesman Jaan Poska (1866-1920). The palace servants lived in the tiny houses on this street. Kadriorg did not develop into just a residential area, but into a summer resort, where wealthy citizens built their fancy summer residences. The tsar's summer palace popularised the area amongst the local and St. Petersburg aristocracy, who came to the Kadriorg curative waters in the warm summer months. Holiday making here became especially popular at the beginning of the 19th century and many of the villas date back to that period.

The construction of wooden buildings in Tallinn intensified at the end of the 19th century, when many people in search of work moved to the town from the countryside. Most of the buildings were inexpensive two-storey rental houses, with stone firewalls between them and vegetable gardens in the back yard, separated from the street by fences. More impressive apartment buildings with a stone stairway, the so-called Tallinn houses, were built in the 1930s. Several modern apartment houses have recently been built here as well.

↖ *Embassy of the Holy See.*

↖ *Old and new apartment houses on the street named after the statesman J. Vilms (1889-1918).*

‹ *Museum of the writer A. H. Tammsaare (1878-1940).*

The Song Festival Grounds were built as a site for all-Estonian song celebrations. Every five years the best choir singers, musicians and folk dancers from Estonia gather here on the first weekend in July. The two-day celebration begins with a festive procession of the participants, most of who are dressed in national costumes. For two days the biggest choir in the world, with about 30 000 singers, performs to an audience reaching two hundred thousand. In between the song festivals, other festivals, fairs, exhibitions and similar events are organised here.

˅ *Song Festival.*
  Thousands of spectators in the foreground
  and choirs on the stage in the background.

The first song festival was held in Tartu in 1869. Since then, song festivals have had a political significance for the Estonian people. In the second half of the 20th century, the song festival was one of the few opportunities to feel spiritually free behind the iron curtain. Participation in the song festival was a matter of pride, and the number of singers increased every year. A new and bigger stage was built in 1960. The song festival flame is lit in the nearby tower. Nowadays a bronze statue of the famous choir conductor Gustav Ernesaks (1908-1993) is located on the slope of the grounds.

Statue of the famous Estonian conductor ⋅ and composer Gustav Ernesaks on the slope of the Song Festival Grounds.

The Song Festival Grounds became one of the places where demonstrations were held at the end of the Soviet era. People started to gather here during the white June nights of 1988 to sing patriotic songs. The desire for freedom was so great at the time that it united the whole nation for a common goal. Hundreds of thousands of people gathered here in a mass demonstration at the beginning of September of the same year, and it was here that the first public calls for the restoration of Estonian independence were made. As song was the only weapon available at the time, that decisive period is known as the Singing Revolution. In the 19th century, at the time of the national awakening, Estonians sang themselves into existence as a European nation. At the end of the 20th century, during the second awakening period, this was repeated when the nation again sang itself to freedom through the tradition of the song festivals.

The idea of the song festivals was taken from the German culture and neighbours were also inspired. Song celebrations today take place in Latvia and Lithuania too. In 2003, the Baltic tradition of song and dance festivals was included in the list of UNESCO Masterpieces of the Oral and Intangible Heritage of Humanity.

Pirita is one of the best loved residential and leisure areas, especially thanks to a long sandy stretch of beach with warm, shallow water. It is possible to do water sports here, and the illuminated skiing and hiking trails under the pines of the woods are well used. The glacial valley of the Pirita River with erratic boulders and sandstone outcrops offers picturesque views for romantics.

Pirita became known worldwide as the host of the sailing regatta of the XXII summer Olympic games in Moscow. Although many countries boycotted the games, they were important to Estonia both politically and economically. Today the Olympic village is still in use, the old buildings have had a facelift, and now a hotel, offices, a swimming pool, a yachting club and a harbour are located here.

The area got its name from the Bridgettine convent, the construction of which was started only a few decades after the convent in Vadstena, Sweden, was consecrated, and almost a decade after Bridget was canonised. Three wealthy Tallinn merchants supported the founding of the convent and it was completed in 1436, gaining fame quickly and becoming the biggest in the region. The convent of St. Bridget was intended for both nuns and monks and was led by an abbess. Although the convent was ruined in the course of the Livonian war in the 16th century, the walls of the church still decorate the centre of Pirita. A new convent was built next to the old one in 2001 and the Order of the Most Holy Saviour of Saint Bridget operates here again.

*St. Bridget's Convent,
centuries old stone crosses in the foreground.*

Arial view of Pirita.

The wood behind the convent is called Kloostrimets (Convent Wood) and under its pines is the Metsakalmistu (Woodland Cemetery), where many famous Estonians – actors and actresses, writers, artists, sporting heroes, government leaders and others – have found their last resting place.

The 314-metre TV-tower completed for the Olympic games is also located here. It is the tallest construction in Estonia, and only a few metres shorter than the highest hill. Its panorama platform at 170 metres is the highest in the Nordic countries; from this height, Tallinn is laid out like a map, and in clear weather the coast of Finland is visible; during the Soviet era the view of the *West* attracted people to visit the tower.

Tallinn TV-tower. ▴

Sailing-boats on the Pirita River, ▾
St. Bridget's Convent in the background.

A unique view of the town is offered from the Pirita road and for many centuries it has been the source of inspiration for artists. Thanks to the beautiful view, a summer manor was built on the slope here at the end of the 17th century, during a boom for construction of summer cottages. The estate changed owners several times and each of them gave it a new name. One of the last owners, count Anatoli Orlov-Davydov from St. Petersburg named the place Mary's Hill (Maarjamäe) in honour of his wife. The magnificent stairs of the 19th century manor originally led straight to the beach. Today they lead to the seaside Pirita road, which was built in 1928 on land reclaimed from the sea, and made even wider for the 1980 Olympic games.

Several monuments are located on the Pirita road, the most beautiful of which is the statue of an angel high up on a granite base, completed in 1902 to commemorate the battleship "Russalka". The base of the monument represents a ship and the more roughly carved stones surrounding it symbolise the waves. Amandus Adamson (1855-1929), the first professional sculptor of Estonian origin, designed the statue.

Orlov Palace, currently the history museum.

Statue of Russalka.

The biggest development in construction of housing units took place during the Soviet era. The area of the town expanded considerably during this period, and the population grew from a couple of hundred thousand before the war to over half a million. After the war, apartment blocks were built in the town centre and private houses on the outskirts. In order to eliminate the shortage of living space, a huge building boom began in the 1960s. The first region to be completed was the residential suburb of Mustamäe, one of Tallinn's biggest, built in a style which was totally different from the existing building traditions. In addition to standard five and nine storey houses, blocks with 14 and 16 floors were built - the highest in Estonia at the time. In the 70s the construction work continued in Õismäe and in the 80s in Lasnamäe. However, the development of these monotonous concrete blocks in Mustamäe, Õismäe and Lasnamäe, the so-called hills (*mäe* comes from the Estonian word meaning "hill"), tended to increase immigration from other republics of the Soviet Union rather than solve the housing problems of the local residents.

⏵ Bird's eye view of Lasnamäe.

NÕMME

Nõmme, a forest town, is one of the most prestigious districts of the capital. The highest hills in Tallinn are here and because of these, Nõmme is the best-liked winter-sports area for the town's inhabitants. The dune coppice became popular already a century ago, and gradually summer cottages were built here. In 1926 Nõmme was granted city rights and within barely a decade it had become the fifth biggest town in Estonia. At the start of the Soviet era, in 1940, it was incorporated into the capital.

When the Nõmme station on the Tallinn-Paldiski railway was opened in 1872, the townspeople began making outings here. At the time the area was owned by the Baltic-German landowner Nikolai von Glehn (1841-1923), who keenly favoured its development. As manor-lands could not be divided and sold as building lots back then, he started renting the land for summer cottages. He rented the first lot on October 6, 1873, with the words, "Let there be a town here."

Castle completed in 1886 to the plan of Nikolai von Glehn.

The first cottages built in Nõmme were small, with a few rooms and a modern glass veranda. Glehn, who was a romantic, built himself a big stone house with a tower in 1886, which is still known as the Glehn Castle. He surrounded it with a park, which, in addition to a palm house and an observatory, was home to a fairy-dragon and the Estonian epic hero Kalevipoeg (Son of Kalev).

Glehn built the town on his land according to his own views. The meticulously detailed building plan took into account both class and national distinctions, so part of the area was inhabited by Germans and part by wealthier Estonians. In sixty years Glehn's dream had come true – the hills covered with pine forest had become a town with all its amenities. The town had a fully functioning local government, established infrastructure, its own newspaper, post-office, several schools, radio and railway stations, market, theatre, cinema, and a museum. In 1934 a ski jump was built on Tallinn's highest hill and in 1936 a spring-water swimming pool was opened.

↟ *Nõmme railway station.*

◂ *Winter in Nõmme.*

◂ *Statue of Kalevipoeg.*

Baron Arthur Girard de Soucanton gave the name Rocca al Mare to this area of former summer estates. As he had a soft spot for Italy he gave the roads and tracks around his summerhouse Italian names and called the whole area Rocca al Mare after the boulders in the sea. Of the summer manor houses only the so-called "Swiss villa" still exists and nowadays the office of the Open Air Museum is located there.

The Open Air Museum was founded in Rocca al Mare in 1957 to display buildings demonstrating country-life from all around Estonia. The oldest exhibit is a chapel from Sutlepa village built in 1699, but most of the buildings in the collection date back to the period 1700 - 1900. A characteristic farm building

Sutlepa chapel.

Well and store-houses in an Estonian farmyard.